T0034581

MARVEL

Can The HULK Lift a HOUSE?

MARVEL

Can The HULK Lift a HOUSE?

Written by Melanie Scott

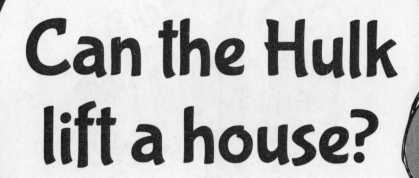

Can the Hulk lift a house?

Yes, he can! The Hulk is so strong, he once lifted a **mountain**! And watch out—as he gets angrier, he gets even **stronger**!

Where is *Black Widow* from ❓

Black Widow—real name **Natasha Romanoff**—is from **Russia**. She used to be an enemy of the Avengers, but now she is on their side.

What would Black Widow be if she were not a Super Hero?

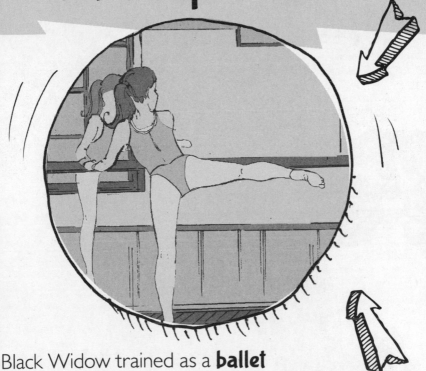

Black Widow trained as a **ballet dancer** when she was a little girl, so maybe she would be a famous ballerina if she were not a Super Hero.

Can Ant–Man talk to ants?

Ant-Man's special **helmet** helps him understand the sounds ants make, and 'talk' to them in their own way. When he is small he can ride on ants.

Who is Ant–Man's daughter?

Ant-Man has a daughter named **Cassie**, whom he loves very much. Cassie has a Super Hero suit that lets her change size just like her dad.

No. Black Panther's claws are part of his Super Hero **costume**. They are made from a special metal called **Vibranium**, which is very strong.

Can Captain Marvel fly?

Captain Marvel can fire energy blasts from her hands!

Yes, Captain Marvel can fly using her **powers**. She also knows how to pilot a plane, and even some alien spaceships!

What's the story with Captain Marvel's cat?

Captain Marvel had a pet cat named **Chewie**. But Chewie was really an alien with lots of tentacles, called a **Flerken**.

What's so special about Thor's hammer?

Thor's hammer is so special it has its own name: **Mjolnir (muh–yol–nir)**. The hammer was made by dwarves from a magical metal called **Uru**.

14

Thor can use the power of his **mind**
to call his hammer back to him. He
can also use it to control **lightning**!

When was Captain America born?

Captain America was
born way back in **1922**.
His birthday is **July 4**,
which is also a big holiday
in the United States of
America. It is called
Independence Day.

Who is Captain America's best friend?

Captain America is good friends with Sam Wilson, who is also known as the Falcon, but his best friend is **Bucky Barnes**. Bucky met Captain America when they were both in the army.

Is Drax an alien?

He looks like an alien now, but Drax used to be a **human** called **Arthur Douglas**. An alien gave him a new, super-strong body so that he could fight powerful enemies like Thanos.

Does Drax have another talent as well as fighting?

Drax plays the **saxophone**! When he was human Drax was very good at playing the instrument, and he can still do it.

Black Panther is the king of a country in Africa
called **Wakanda**. His real name is T'Challa.
There are lots of clever scientists and inventors
in Wakanda, but they keep their inventions secret.

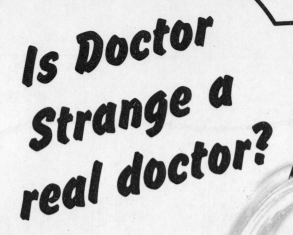

Is Doctor Strange a real doctor?

Yes. Before he became Master of the Mystic Arts, Doctor Strange worked in a hospital. He was a top **surgeon**, but he hurt his hands in a car accident and couldn't do his job any more.

Who is Gamora's dad?

Gamora is the adopted daughter of **Thanos**, one of the biggest baddies around. She is not a villain like her dad, but is one of the good guys.

Thanos

Why does Gamora have green skin?

Gamora is from an alien planet called **Zen–Whoberi**. Everyone who comes from Zen-Whoberi has green skin, just like Gamora.

Can Falcon talk to birds?

He has a falcon called **Redwing** that he can talk to using just his mind. This is called **telepathy**. He can also control other birds and see what they see as they fly.

Can Falcon fly?

Yes. He cannot fly on his own, but he has **metal wings** on his costume. Black Panther gave the wings to Falcon.

What is Hawkeye's super-power?

Hawkeye does not have a super-power like his Avenger friends, but he is very brave and brilliant with a **bow** and **arrow**. He has lots of 'trick' arrows that do different things like explode or help him swing between buildings.

Does Hawkeye have a pet?

Yes. Hawkeye has a dog called **Lucky** whom he rescued from a gang of bad guys. Lucky's favorite food is **pizza**!

Is Shuri a *princess?*

One of Shuri's amazing gadgets

Yes. Shuri is a **princess** of Wakanda. She helps to protect Wakanda with her brother, the **Black Panther**.

What is Shuri's greatest skill?

Shuri is very **clever**. She loves science and **inventing** cool gadgets.

Where does Doctor Strange live?

Sanctum Sanctorum

Doctor Strange has a house called the Sanctum Sanctorum in Greenwich Village, **New York City**. He keeps all his cool magical objects there, like the Cloak of Levitation.

Cloak of Levitation

Doctor Strange's special **cloak** helps him fly.

37

How powerful is *Scarlet Witch?*

Scarlet Witch is one of the most powerful Avengers ever. Her magic can do almost **anything**.

Does Scarlet Witch have a family?

Quicksilver

She has a twin brother, the super-speedy Super Hero named **Quicksilver**.

How did Sam Alexander become Nova?

He found his dad's **Nova helmet**, which gave him lots of cool powers. Then Gamora and Rocket Raccoon taught him how to use it.

How does Nova relax?

Sam likes watching **sports** and listening to **music**. He also enjoys eating candy bars!

What does Rocket Raccoon do for fun?

Rocket loves to **fix** things. He is very good at taking machines apart and making them even better than before.

How tall is Rocket Raccoon?

Rocket is about **3 feet tall**, or **91 cm**. That's about the same as an Emperor penguin.

How old is *Thor?*

Thor is from **Asgard**, a place where people live for a very long time. He was around at the time of the Vikings, so he is more than **1,000 years old**. That's a lot of birthday candles!

What does Spider-Man eat ?

He does not eat bugs and flies like a spider!
He eats lots of food that many teenagers like
to eat. Peter Parker's favorite treat is a New
York-style **hot dog**.

When you are Spider-Man,
it's easy to find a quiet place
to enjoy a snack.

What happens to *the Hulk's* clothes when he gets bigger?

Hulk's real name is **Bruce Banner**. When Bruce becomes the Hulk, he gets really big and most of his clothes **tear**. Bruce has designed a pair of special pants that stretch as he grows and keep him covered up.

The Hulk doesn't seem to **mind** the cold!

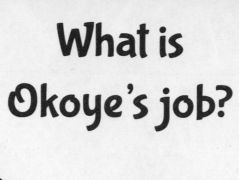

What is Okoye's job?

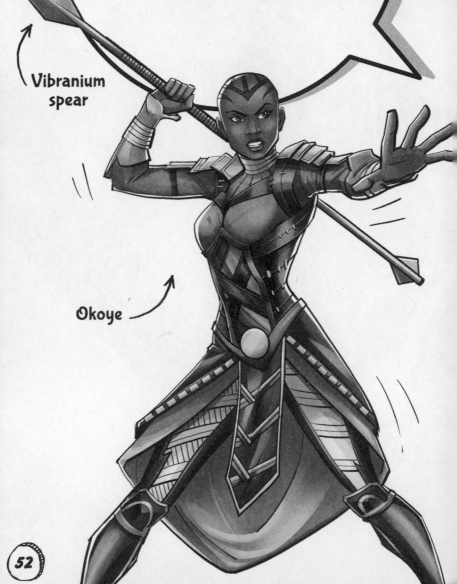

Vibranium
spear

Okoye

Okoye leads a group of female guards
called the **Dora Milaje**. These guards
protect the king or queen of Wakanda.
They are very strong and brave.

Dora Milaje

Which Iron Man armor is the **strongest?**

Iron Man's suits are all very strong, but the biggest and strongest is the **Hulkbuster** armor. This suit was built to stop the mighty Hulk if he gets out of control.

What is Iron Man's favorite music?

Let's rock 'n' roll!

Iron Man is a big fan of **rock music**. This type of music can also be called '**heavy metal**' —like Iron Man's armor!

Is Nebula a robot?

Nebula is not a robot, but some of her body is made from **metal**. This makes her really strong.

What is Nebula's job?

Nebula does not have a job like regular people—she is a kind of **space pirate**.

Does Miles Morales have the same powers as Peter Parker?

Although Miles and Peter are both Spider-Man, their powers are a bit different.

As well as **crawling** on walls and making **webs** like a spider, Miles can fire **electric** blasts and **camouflage** himself.

Who is Miles Morales's best friend?

Miles's best friend is named **Ganke Lee**. They are such good friends that Miles can trust him with a secret: he is Spider-Man!

Is **Groot** a tree?

No. Groot is a **Flora colossus**, a type of alien that looks a bit like a tree. Like a walking, talking tree!

Why is Mantis a good friend?

Mantis can tell when people are feeling **happy**, **sad**, or **angry**—that's her super-power! She knows when someone needs help, even if they do not say anything.

What is Mantis's talent?

Mantis is good at lots of things, but her best talent is **martial arts**. She is very hard to beat in a battle because she is quick on her feet.

What is the Rainbow Bridge?

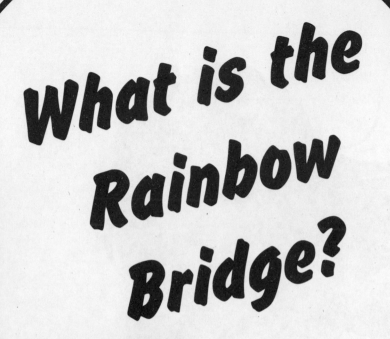

Heimdall

The Rainbow Bridge, or **Bifrost**, is what the **Asgardians** use to travel to other places. It is guarded by **Heimdall**.

What is Ms. Marvel's power?

Ms. Marvel can change her body shape in lots of ways. She can make herself larger or smaller, and is very **stretchy**.

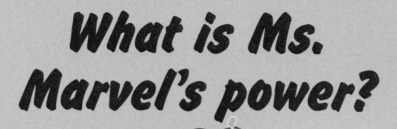

68

Who is Ms. Marvel's favorite Super Hero?

Ms. Marvel is a big fan of lots of Super Heroes, but her favorite is **Captain Marvel** (Carol Danvers). That is why she chose the Super Hero name Ms. Marvel.

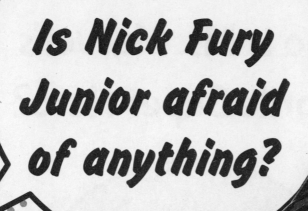

Is Nick Fury Junior afraid of anything?

Nick Fury Junior leads **S.H.I.E.L.D.**, a group of Super Heroes that protects the world from harm.

As the team's leader, Nick must stay calm in scary situations. He is rarely rattled—not even by an angry Hulk!

Who is Nick Fury Junior's best friend?

When Nick Fury Junior was in the army he made friends with **Phil Coulson**, whose nickname was 'Cheese.' Later, Fury and Coulson worked together at S.H.I.E.L.D.

Who is stronger—Iron Man or War Machine?

Iron Man VS.

War Machine's armor is **stronger** and has more guns than Iron Man's, but it is not as **fast**. However, Iron Man and War Machine are best friends. They always work together.

War Machine

Does Odin take naps?

Yes! Every year, Odin needs to take a long nap called the **Odinsleep** so that his powers stay strong. He can sleep for a week!

What are Odin's favorite animals?

Odin has clever **ravens** and **wolves** who work for him. He also rides a **horse**—with eight legs!

Does She–Hulk know the Hulk?

Yes, they are **cousins**.
She-Hulk can change
back to a normal human
when she wants, but she
enjoys being She-Hulk.
She likes to be strong
and powerful!

What is She–Hulk's job?

As well as fighting for justice as a Super Hero, She-Hulk also protects the innocent as a **lawyer**.

Is Star-Lord an alien?

That's half true!
Star-Lord's real
name is **Peter Quill**.
His mother is from Earth,
but his father is an alien king
from a planet called **Spartax**.

Yes. He has a small **device** on his neck that helps him understand all the different alien languages he hears.

Can Star–Lord talk to aliens?

Who built *Vision?*

Vision is a **synthezoid**, which is a type of robot. A villain called **Ultron** created him to fight the Avengers, but Vision did not want to hurt them. He joined the team himself.

Ultron

Does Vision eat and sleep like a human?

He does not need food or sleep, but Vision can **eat** and **drink** with his teammates if he wants to feel more like a real human.

Why does Groot only say "I am Groot"?

I am Groot!

Rocket

To most people it sounds like he is only saying "I am Groot," but Groot is really saying lots of things in his own **language**. Luckily his best friend **Rocket** can understand him!

Is the Wasp small all the time?

No. The Wasp is usually the size of other humans, but she can **shrink** whenever she wants to. She can also **grow** very big.

Does the Wasp sting?

Yes. The Wasp can fire **electric** 'stings' from her hands.

What does Heimdall do in Asgard?

Heimdall is the Sentry of Asgard. This means he helps **guard** it from danger. He is good at this because he can **see**, **hear**, and even **smell** better than anybody else in Asgard.

What is the coolest thing about War Machine's suit?

War Machine can make his armor **blend** in with what is around him—just like a type of lizard called a chameleon!

Powerful machine gun

Suit provides superhuman strength.

Glossary

Asgardians People who come from the mystical world of Asgard.

Avengers A group of Super Heroes who defend Earth from attacks.

camouflage Colors, patterns, or shapes that help someone blend in with their surroundings.

device An item that has been built to help with a task.

inventor A person who has ideas for new items.

justice Fair treatment and behavior.

language A particular way of communicating using words.

lawyer A person who understands the law and helps people to fight unfair treatment or actions.

lightning An electrical release of energy that usually comes with a flash of light and a rumbling sound called thunder.

martial art A form of combat, such as karate. Martial arts are also a form of self-defense and can be practiced as a sport.

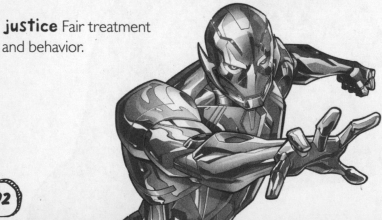

saxophone A metal instrument which is played by blowing into it.

scientist A person who studies science and solves problems by doing experiments.

surgeon A medical professional who can perform operations.

synthezoid A robot that has been created to mimic the human body.

telepathy The ability to read other people's minds and communicate without speech.

tentacles Long, bendy parts of an animal that are used to grab hold of things.

Vikings
People who lived in Scandinavia more than 1,000 years ago. They are famous for taking long sea journeys to distant lands and for being fierce warriors.

Index

Project Editor Pamela Afram
Project Art Editor Stefan Georgiou
Senior Designer Nathan Martin
Senior Production Editor Jennifer Murray
Senior Production Controller Louise Minihane
Managing Editor Sarah Harland
Managing Art Editor Vicky Short
Publishing Director Mark Searle

First American Edition, 2021
Published in the United States
by DK Publishing, 1450 Broadway,
Suite 801, New York, NY 10018

Page design Copyright © 2021
Dorling Kindersley Limited
DK, a Division of Penguin
Random House LLC
21 22 23 24 25 10 9 8 7 6 5 4 3 2 1
001–321719–Apr/2021

© 2021 MARVEL

A catalog record for this
book is available from the
Library of Congress.

ISBN 978-0-7440-2728-0
(Paperback)
ISBN 978-0-7440-3128-7
(Hardcover)

DK books are available at special
discounts when purchased
in bulk for sales promotions,
premiums, fund-raising, or
educational use. For details,
contact: DK Publishing Special
Markets, 1450 Broadway,
Suite 801, New York, NY 10018
SpecialSales@dk.com

Printed in China

For the curious

www.dk.com

This book is made from
Forest Stewardship Council™
certified paper—one small
step in DK's commitment
to a sustainable future.